How To Find All Missing Persons / Unsolved Cases. And Collect All Reward Offers. Volume XXXIV. THE CASE OF MARIA SMITH REAL NAME MARIA STERT

DAVID GOMADZA

www.twofuture.world

Copyright © 2024 David Gomadza

All rights reserved.

Paperback ISBN: 9798328111737

DEDICATION

To a better future.

CONTENTS

How To Find All Missing Persons /
Unsolved Cases.
And Collect All Reward Offers. Volume XXXIV
THE CASE OF MARIAH SMITH
REAL NAME MARIA STERT   1

The Afterlife Conversation

and The Court Of Creation.   7

The Killers.   25

ACKNOWLEDGMENTS

Tomorrow's World Order

How To Find All Missing Persons / Unsolved Cases. And Collect All Reward Offers. Volume XXXIV. THE CASE OF MARIA SMITH REAL NAME MARIA STERT

BACKGROUND INFORMATION

The NSW Government has announced a $1 million reward for information that leads to a conviction over the 1974 murder of a young Eastern Suburbs woman.

The body of 20-year-old Maria Smith was located in the bedroom of her unit on St Marks Road, Randwick, in the early evening of Monday 22 April 1974.

Maria had been bound, sexually assaulted and strangled with pantyhose.

Maria's husband, Stephen, had left for work just after 7.30am and she was meant to leave about an hour later for work, but never arrived.

Despite extensive investigations and a Coronial Inquest in July 1975, which found that she had been strangled by an unknown person, no one was charged in connection to her murder.

The Homicide Squad's Unsolved Homicide Unit has established Strike Force Auris to reinvestigate the circumstances surrounding Maria's death.

As investigations continue, the NSW Government has announced a $1 million reward for information that leads Strike Force Auris investigators to those responsible for Maria's murder.

NSW Minister for Police Troy Grant said this is the first time a $1

How To Find All Missing Persons / Unsolved Cases. And Collect All Reward Offers.
Volume XXXIII. THE CASE OF MARIA SMITH REAL NAME MARIA STERT

million reward has been offered since the new rewards system was announced in December 2017.

"No matter how long a case goes unsolved, the family and friends of the victim have to live with their grief as well as the knowledge that justice has not been served," Mr Grant said.

"Under the new system investigations involving the most serious offences, such as murder, can have a maximum $1 million reward in order to generate renewed public interest in the case and prompt fresh information that could lead to an arrest."

Homicide Squad Commander, Detective Superintendent Scott Cook, welcomed the reward, which he hopes will be the catalyst for someone to come forward with information that will help provide justice for Maria.

"Maria's murder had an incredible impact on the community at the time, but it is nothing compared to the suffering her family have endured over the last 44 years," Det Supt Cook said.

"She had only been married eight weeks and, at the age of 20, had her whole life ahead of her.

Peter McGuinn, who was just a young man when his sister was murdered, said it was difficult to describe the impact losing Maria had on his family.

"From that day, it was like there's a void that couldn't – and can't – be filled," Mr McGuinn said.

"Even after 44 years, we still think about Maria often, mostly it's our childhood memories and what could have been, but other times, I think about what actually happened – who killed my sister?

"Even though our parents have passed without that answer, we know that someone knows who did it and hope that this reward is encouragement to come forward and tell the police," Mr McGuinn

How To Find All Missing Persons / Unsolved Cases. And Collect All Reward Offers.
Volume XXXIII. THE CASE OF MARIA SMITH REAL NAME MARIA STERT

said.

Det Supt Cook said at the time of the murder, investigators had a number of possible theories about the motives of Maria's killer, including links to the murder of Lynette White.

"Having reviewed both cases, we are now conducting separate investigations into each of these matters," Det Supt Cook said.

"That said, we are keeping an open mind and welcome any information from the community that may assist our inquiries and help bring us closer to providing answers to both families.

"Investigators are seeking to re-interview various people who were in contact with Maria at the time, including friends, work colleagues, and even those she may have spoken to while working at Malabar RSL Club.

"In particular, Strike Force Auris investigators would like to speak to anyone who lived in the Smith's unit block – 14-20 St Marks Road – in early 1974.

"The passage of time makes tracking everyone down difficult, so we appeal for anyone who may have spoken to the original investigators to get in touch again now.

"Obviously we are keen to speak to anyone who has information about Maria's murder, and we urge them to contact us as soon as possible," Det Supt Cook said.

Police are urging anyone with information that may assist Strike Force Auris investigators to call Crime Stoppers on 1800 333 000 or use the Crime Stoppers online reporting page: https://nsw.crimestoppers.com.au/ Information you provide will be treated in the strictest of confidence. We remind people they should not report crime information via our social media pages.

https://www.police.nsw.gov.au/can_you_help_us/rewards/1000000_r

How To Find All Missing Persons / Unsolved Cases. And Collect All Reward Offers. Volume XXXIII. THE CASE OF MARIA SMITH REAL NAME MARIA STERT

eward/$1_million_nsw_government_reward_announced_for_information_into_1974_murder_of_maria_smith

TOMORROW'S WORLD ORDER'S PERSPECTIVES

USE OF PREDEFINED AFTERLIFE PARAMETERS

These guide souls the moment it exist the human body on its journey to Yahweh the creator these define what to do and what to expect as you go to hell or heaven if a souk leaves earth it enters ozone orbit and instantly everything reboots for it to start a new phase of life after living the earth's body now what happens is that it enters the ozone orbit and a simply click caused by the sudden drop of pressure from -1186 to – 20 means the bottom shaft of the soul will lift rapidly and this pushes its back into the air higher than its head best example is a penguin but with real human legs and head just the shape now God created a life predefined program for them instead of asking what should I do and where should I go they instantly know from predefined stencils if you did well and talked most about God then heaven is for you if you did evil and talked more about the devil then the devil is yours now if we Ask what can be of humans without souks this is the answer dead forever your soul is you a new transformation to the electromagnetic waves life where you see Yahweh for the first time and praise him and wish you had seen him a long time ago because of his Majesty and will always be there forever now what are all these you may ask these are rules to be guided by in the creation court in short it has everything humans know about the judges and the presiding judge who will always be Yahweh and 84 angels surrounding the altar 28 high priests who always say Yahweh have mercy on humans and 74 smaller courts priests who always say Yahweh has mercy on humans and 96 princesses who say glory to Yahweh forever and ever amen we have 96 elders who always say if I can why he can't meaning if the devil can drink blood why can't Yahweh who created the devil and blood do the same now this is not the same as saying if the devil can kill why can Yahweh its more on professional grounds rather than challenging now if we look at the inside of the court we have 81 priests surrounding the altar who say Yahweh be merciful to humans but if they disobey you we put hem on trial for you and kill them for you almighty Yahweh inside this is a round circle where Yahweh sits and asks questions now if we look deep inside the court you will see that there are other things that resemble earth high courts like

benches and chairs 10 times human sizes for the gods who are so enormous 2 are equal to 84 billion humans in size
predefined parameters for humans after death as in know what is inside is a large size of books the book of creation is among them with 10897867892836789012348678901245861789011 pages and is divided into humans first then chapter for animals then a chapter for angles then a chapter for gods and a chapter for Joseph Yahweh's best friend and a chapter for Yahweh's best friend's wife Anna and a chapter for Yahweh's wife Catitighit and lastly a chapter for Yahweh and recently a chapter for davidgomadza as Yahweh's representative on earth marking the new beginnings starting in 2025

1. tell us who killed you
2. tell us what killed you
3. tell us why and who killed you
4. tell us why you died
5. tell us what could have been done and is not done
6. tell us what could be and why
7. tell is when this happened
8. tell us why this is so
9. tell us why this is so
10. what can be done to improve this

What does the book of creation say about davidgomadza David Gomadza is the first and last ruler to be appointed by Yahweh fir the next 25 billion years and will act as his representative on earth deciding cases and upholding his principles on earth and as such has been entitled to 489 trillion dollars in assets this number signifies eternity among humans and the beginning of a new Era chapter 78678928028938628418902876890183208678901234867890182364 87289128610 Creation manual the new Era of new electromagnetic wave conduit signed and dated by Yahweh himself on 27may2024 at 237800 Yatime
creation.universe.ya.start.end.find.davidgomadza.ya.askya.ya

Ask.read.creation.manucreation.universe.ya.start.end.find.davidgoma askya.ya

How To Find All Missing Persons / Unsolved Cases. And Collect All Reward Offers. Volume XXXIII. THE CASE OF MARIA SMITH REAL NAME MARIA STERT

Ask.rulesofthecourt.start.now.start
David Gomadza welcome the rules of court are guiding principles that tell you what to do and how to do it first you must always say I believe in the court of creation and I shall abide by he rules of this court and shall always do things according to the rules of this court in deciding the cases I am assigned to you must ask what can be done so that you know all your options before making choices the court system will make it easy to check files and ask the outcomes of the decision ask the court the final decision in any case.

THE AFTERLIFE CONVERSATION AND THE COUNCIL OF CREATION'S ANAYLSIS.

god here me i was attacked violently by asorop mnope who said what can be of homeless orphans with no one to ask for anything but god when god can't be reached by phone and i said i talk to god all the time so what does a phone have to do with god and he said i can't make you talk to him if you want and he said i can ask him for you right now and he put his hands together and said god this you woman wants to know if you can help her with paying out rent after all she is the landlord as it turned but what can she do when no one wants to pay to a teenager for that matter and he took out 100 dollar bill ad paid as his rent but he must 250 and i said if you can't pay then move out i can't ask everyday from you money but he said i will not just now i said i want 150 by tomorrow or i give you back this and you move out so he agreed then the next day he said if i can i will and left but did not get back until 8pm at night when house office will have closed at 7pm then because i wanted him to pay or move out that day so he asked what can be of young teens with no income but own large properties and he said can make everyone else move out so that you can't afford and he said who said i can't pay i will get a loan and pay but he laughed and i said if you can then the court can throw you out okay i said mind your business just pay okay he agreed and paid 250 and said now that is my turn i paid you 100 pounds extra so i want sex with you right now and no buts nothing you pressed so much fir a 100 dollar bill you got it now open your legs let's start but i took only 150 and walked out if i am your landlord makes no sense

How To Find All Missing Persons / Unsolved Cases. And Collect All Reward Offers.
Volume XXXIII. THE CASE OF MARIA SMITH REAL NAME MARIA STERT

i give you sex next day i give him notice 1 month and he moved out but the next day and i refunded minus 1 day stay so i gave him 241 dollars and took 9 dollars for one day then he accepted and left fearing i call police but he went there and said i got kicked out after complaining she want sex but can't say then she said i am your landlord and he sat at the police for 8 months saving money so i guessed but they had somehow recorded our conversation and when i saw him he was so bitter he nearly attacked me in the street and said you owe me 100 dollars or he touched his genitals now having grown up a little bit i started to understand what they were saying that i ought to be making money as well to put aside so i don't loose the house so i said give me the 100 i give you the sex but once and never again but he was broke he said i will make the 100 and then get back to you and i said only now and never talk about this forever but god i died i killed a girl called maria stoert meaning masterton she said what can i do for you but and left and came back and said i can but and left and said if i can i will but then never returned so i thought she needed sex why did you kill her the police said i can give you 5% of the value of the house in 5 years or 8 per cent of the value in 8 years

i am aty for maria sterty but they told me her real name is maria astert because she own a house she must be killed on 22 april 1974 exactly this i knew on her day of birth and she said i want my father eric asert to be here my dad come back daddy come daddy so i cried too for the first time and said from today i am your daddy but she said no god i want you to be god then it said i want to ask you a question and i said yes and it said what can be said of orphans with property worth a million and no income and he said i can but hoe much and he said 5 in 5 or 8 but in 5 but then and stopped then she said i can if you can but then stopped by the time he said it's okay i realised she was not thinking about sex at all so the police put me in jail for 8 months on good behaviour but when i come out then they said you did time spread but she hasn't now she can pay you in advance sex then you pay her later that's how things works and said if i can then she can and when i saw her she has been eating a lot and had changed to be a lovely woman then she said i can give you sex

How To Find All Missing Persons / Unsolved Cases. And Collect All Reward Offers. Volume XXXIII. THE CASE OF MARIA SMITH REAL NAME MARIA STERT

but now after serving time i don't want sex with you anymore if it leads to this serving time without touching you what if i touch you then what long prison sentence i said i did not report you and he said i know but you did you have an aty and i said what aty then i did not know i just knew like now about this aty i thought this was god asorop mnope is called asorop mstert who killed a young teenager called maria smith but real name maria stert who owned the most expensive renting accommodation at the time kicking out those who can't pay and then said if none can pay then what i can reduce it affects the value of the house and then what to do after that now if we ask what can be done about this then this is the answer she can ask for more now if we look at this case then she is the most expensive landlord but never had problems because people rented there out of sympathy and most knew the parents and how they died they had drowned when
they went swimming now what is interesting is this she worked
i am pc astert mnopt real name stuvert stopert i work for the police department in queenslands i put capital gains tax on all property in queensland and go after that house until we have taken it now i ask any lord lord to start paying in advance monthly so that when they sell the house they don't have to pay so i asked this teenager maria shert to pay and she said she will check with her lawyer who turns out to be her brother who said that's a lie and i got kicked out of the property now i ask what can be of people with the best villas in town but who can't pay for them then this is the answer they can be taken as well now what can you say about maria how did she die according to you astonop had a job to do kill her we cover for you for 20 years then you come back and say i know who killed her it was god she died of cancer and get the reward but deposit 40% into the fund the police account then go to an account called setrtet and say i want to add s deposit then deposit 90000 then go to an account called avert then deposit 90000 then go to an account called averty deposit 90000 then go to an account called asert ajen and deposit 90000 then go to an account called asert and deposit 90000 then ask for police housing association and deposit the rest but now you see what is happening is that you don't have anything left for you now then deposit your 90000 into an account of your choice and send us the account

How To Find All Missing Persons / Unsolved Cases. And Collect All Reward Offers.
Volume XXXIII. THE CASE OF MARIA SMITH REAL NAME MARIA STERT

number then ask us how can i be of any help to society we check you then offer you a job to solve crime with us then in the end after another 20 years you will have a million dollars
i see why they advisories $1million its to repay everyone helping to cover and remove all the evidence from sight so that everyone get a share of every reward offered meaning there are no rewards as rewards but crooks feeding their pockets
it is a murder and coverup syndicate of 90000 dollar rounds for every reward offered with the chance to open your own account and start earning as well but you must wait until 20 years to make a million meaning they need to kill and take at least 20 houses meaning 20 cold cases per year per county x 100 to make a million in 20 years meaning 9 cases must go as cold cases per each time now looking at these cases it start to make sense that these cases are just not to be solved and must be written as cold cases so that the money syndicate goes on if stopped then the money will not flow this year as it has done for the past 54 years since this 1 million dollar syndicate club started if we calculate meaning a total of 28698360 minus value of the first 20 years when there is nothing which means 2728924 has been distributed to each account now the number of these 1 million dollar rewards has gone to 64 per county or state in this country australia so all capital gains tax goes to the british queen normally a fraction of the true cost because they lie about the value of the house that's why we have to reduce it first to a quarter then we calculate capital gains tax then issue a notice of collection on that value then filed it as if the house has been paid then after 5 years pay all as a lump sum for that period so they can check and verify all even if they suspect they are asking us to kill children orphans for that matter so what can they do but accept.
god i am dying old now make sure i come to you to heaven that means you can forgive me now but i want you to know that i killed maria stert at her house because i got so drunk i nearly died and said i want sex with you before i die and he said okay then sat on my lap then said i want you to know that i think of you highly but a man must ask what can be done and this is my answer you can always ask her for sex one day she might need this money you waste on alcohol so i said what can be done to make her want me more then it said you

How To Find All Missing Persons / Unsolved Cases. And Collect All Reward Offers.
Volume XXXIII. THE CASE OF MARIA SMITH REAL NAME MARIA STERT

can always ask if she want or not nicely if not then forget about it but you must tell her that you did not mean harm but pleasure so she is not afraid of you but she said i talk to god everyday and he did not say that then i said god i want you to know that i love you and one day we will be together but not yet because i fall in love with a 19 year old and i am 48 years old and if i ask what can be done then this is the answer marry her and make the property always strong by inviting friends to stay that means you can marry each other secretly until you have enough money to pay all your house bills then i agreed but she said i talk to my god and prayed as well that time and said he did not say that he said report him instead to us then walked away that alone made me realize that my best god is so not god after all they are tricking everyone even i growing up argued with priests etc saying there is a god who i can easily talk to and ask questions and asked him in front of you but when she said he said that no but get him arrested instead then it's the police all along i went there angry about them impersonating god then they said we heard everything you nearly molested her so you must go to the court but in the court they said i was drunk and disorderly but i just thought that this was part of the maria case but i spent 8 months locked up only because i had no where to go he said where does he live and said at that expensive house owned by the teenager and the judge said is he making request for sex from her and they said no so i said yes but she is an older woman 19 years i can actual marry her and none of you can say anything but the judge said in that case find new accommodation i prohibit you staying there then he said find another accommodation once you have this accommodation then tell me so that we release you even today but i refused and said i stay there full stop but that cost me 8 months when i was released she said i am grown up now soon i can be 20 years and can enjoy sex for 100 dollars with you but i didn't want because i know that her god is not god but a policeman one who listen all the time i felt betrayed worse humiliated considering all my arguments about god there was no god at least who can speak to humans all this talk about god is the police spying on everyone to make things worse illegally so wrong and confusing that i took my gun and aimed at one of them the other day after sometime i got over it and lived my life until one day a man

How To Find All Missing Persons / Unsolved Cases. And Collect All Reward Offers.
Volume XXXIII. THE CASE OF MARIA SMITH REAL NAME MARIA STERT

came and said can you do the work and l said yes then he wrote a map and drew on it and said you must find this area dig it and find out what you can if not leave it for 2 weeks then close it but said identified as artostuv asertpmnop who said i can but who can dig the grave to put her asking his aty knowing that it would be a policeman on the other end then he said what if we are to kill you instead who would you trade for then he looked around and said any landlord i work just to pay the rent so i can him in his mind he had aropt snonorst who acted as the landlord to give her support and his aty said but its that little girl who is the landlord then he said i can't i have children no one with a child would kill another child so i refuse outright

so he said if i can then anyone can when i looked at him he said i want to live then he left when i asked

i went to find this area and found it and looked at it the only thing was that it was nothing but hidden away from all other place and he said did you find it and i said yes then he offered me 500 but he said 2 months rent and i thought 500 dollars cash and i said the money first but he said you don't understand you must not get cash but free rent for two months i looked at him and instantly said no i will rather fuck her than kill her what do i gain killing the woman you went to jail for expecting not to are you made i want to fuck her but he said she said she can't ever anyone after the neighbour's told everyone that she said if you can't pay rent then have sex and pay with 100 dollars on top for sex next month and he agreed that killed him that he is not special but the same like everyone else so he asked does she have any female tenants

asorop mstert after that i agreed because he said you are not listening two months rent and same when property is sold after 5 years i said i have no 5 years to wait and he said okay for you in 1 because you talk too much and you spent time already then i asked what is it in layman's terms and she suddenly appeared and said i want rent this month double if you can but nothing to worry too much i have been served with the first notice someone gave bond to police instead of me saying i don't trust her and that cost me one moth mortgage and two months i am out of the business forever and the thieves get my father's house i should have listened to you non of this could have

How To Find All Missing Persons / Unsolved Cases. And Collect All Reward Offers.
Volume XXXIII. THE CASE OF MARIA SMITH REAL NAME MARIA STERT

happened i heard a rich man in town is offering people double pay and 5 percent after 5 years who is he and what kind of a job if i was a man i can but i can't then she said if i can i can but then went out and then said if i can i can but then kept quiet now if we can then we can but then what can we do to make up for this then he said i can kill her then you just bury her but confess to god that you killed her so that you get reward at the end and i said what reward and he said there is a reward at the end of 20 years you can collect this to settle in your new house i said what new house he said it's like a syndicate every year a person in that syndicate get a house on his belt through repossession and the other person who did the work will get a house obtained the same but by the others so that it can't be traced to him that means if the syndicate has 8 members at the beginning then 8 orphans must die that period to release 8 houses if say sergent 1 kills or help the house is for sergent 2 and so on now if we look the last person from this group to get a house was pc aoprt who did not kill anyone but opened a fake account by the name asern ajern and got a number and send it to 8 different people then at the end the first pc aoprt then got a house now let's look at the money we know now how the money works if one sends a reward request the money is as follows
1. 90000
2. 90000
3. 90000
4. 90000
5. 90000
6. 180000
7. 700000
this is money from publicity of the case which must reach a target of 8 million dollars and where the 1 million dollars come from
i refused and said i don't want to tarnish myself i love her that much to kill her but i can take the money for protecting the killer then he said what can be said of dirty police who offer to get a child killed for their house even worse an orphan now he said i can but ran after this i can't do time anymore never then he went outside leaving her not knowing or understanding what they are talking about even though he was there then she said what do you men talk about is it

How To Find All Missing Persons / Unsolved Cases. And Collect All Reward Offers.
Volume XXXIII. THE CASE OF MARIA SMITH REAL NAME MARIA STERT

about me god said they are planning to kill you and bury you in the woods where your father said was best for his grave instead since you did not tell people at the funeral maybe you want that place and instantly she remembers her father saying put me here this is the best place here i like it and smiled but then she had no idea what happens on death she thought whole body go to heaven then she sat down and said all this about sex these men would rather kill me to stop others having a good time he said this is not a brothel and she said what is a brothel then she said what brothel this is a housing accommodation house but if sex if there take or leave don't spoil things i just paid two months in advance and she smiled and squeezed her big tips then and left and ran to the police and said all men talk about getting me in a grave for sex is that justified before i didn't want sex they all go to prison running away he stayed 8 months just to avoid his demons asking me for sex now i offer it for 100 then 50 next month 20 dollars per session then all start saying let's dig a grave and kill her they actually told me where to bury me is this right what can you do i asked god and he said go to the police and she looked at them they all said it's hearsay doesn't mean anything i left with nothing then the night of
asorop mnope but mstert...-
the night she died she said i want to ask you a serious question the house is mine then why do the police want to sell it i offer someone extra sex for information and he said i can tell you a secret because you gave me too much and i can't pay then she said why the police what to sell my house when i am alive and still here is this not an attack on an innocent women?
she then said what it do you think the people i pay money can talk to kill me is this right and i said no why they want to kill you she said they want me dead take the house then know that i can't accept dead but sex so if you can't because you are old than everyone else then you go away from me not me dying for an old bastard like you you hide 8 months in prison from me so go back there if you don't have anything to say this time i tell the truth and all about the drunkness and add anything i like about the gun you hide inside the torn pillow he instantly grabbed her by the neck and held her against his body and pushed her down and squeezed for real until death and her

How To Find All Missing Persons / Unsolved Cases. And Collect All Reward Offers.
Volume XXXIII. THE CASE OF MARIA SMITH REAL NAME MARIA STERT

i escape long ago has just started i can't believe from no where to death its so untrue against all predefined parameters and so fast she has 2 seconds to live i just can't believe this is happening she only wanted sex with him but then again he slept on the wrong side of the bed strangulation calculations initiated at 20.00pm queensland time australia she had just bought new lingerie to show off but i guess someone else tipped him off as he was only to look if he try to touch and use her god to call the police after discovering that the police were the ones pretending to be god so furious that she said i take his gun tonight and shot one this is stealing they got my parents killed too the whole family we believed that there is a god how can i trust these surely one must die i understand why he went to prison to try and kill them there

3 seconds she had already died her soul run out way too fast to complete anything but as it turns out everything was already calculated in advance from the day she failed to pay her mortgage she is buried in that pit where her father said i like this place coordinates 08982836789028678902836789028678901283678902848068367890283678901802803 6 at amsort resort 1 mile east and 1mile north of a rock called once you loved me but now you don't in a corner of the area that hidden from the eye you have to neal down to see it

maria smith [stert] but real name maria stonospt after secretly marrying aropt stonospt who strangled her when she threatened to send him to jail after the police took advantage if the situation and sent him to jail just for failing to give an address nothing to do with maria but now realizing that they can do anything they want even illegal things like lying about god she threaten to send him back and knowing how unjust they were he strangled her so he offered her one choice before she dies where do you want to go hell or heaven but she said rebirth

maria

maria smith or stert radar coordinates

all names and people in the world

maria stert the house was owned by maria stert who was 16 at the time of having the house is maria stert her father was eric stert mother was stella montery-stert why maria changed name to smith

How To Find All Missing Persons / Unsolved Cases. And Collect All Reward Offers. Volume XXXIII. THE CASE OF MARIA SMITH REAL NAME MARIA STERT

because of farley imprisoning atopt stonorspt and faked to have married him because the police had locked him in prison for 8 months without committing an offense so she agreed to change name but just for that time until time she get back the house.
coordinates are
08678902836789028468902836789028789027689024578901365820
10987890
south of australia at near a junction called as from you as to you in local language
coordinates 85678902841890283

artostuv asertpmnop was a police officer who said I can if
Did you kill Maria stert / smith no was killed by stonorsp who got afraid of going back to jail and strangled her then buried her in the pit another guy has asked to be dug creating many options that anyone could have dug it and buried her there the coordinates of the pit are
089867890283678906878902683148902841856789023489018567890284190 at aseert ranch near asert belt owned by the victim where there was an expensive house later bought by Pc atopt mrotutet who said I can but did you buy Maria smith house yes and sold it to the astert bank for 2.786482 dollars but before I used the money I lost the paperwork and the check then that night a man followed me and stubbed me to death that same night and was sent to hell.

her real name was maria stert who owns a house with value over 2 million dollars but one she failed to pay once then resulting in the takeover that needed an immediate response and by the night before 21.00pm she was dead a man called asonorpt stonorst killed her by strangulation after she threatened to send him to prison for a crime before having sent him technical for nothing now use that to strangle her with so much rage that the long ago start range gave her3 seconds by the first one her soul had escaped to heaven but she died after 4 minutes rather than the 3 given to her and only said if I can then what and died forever with so much rage that she refused to live the reception…demanding to be sent back for rebirth but Yahweh admitted if he had powers he would send her back this case has

How To Find All Missing Persons / Unsolved Cases. And Collect All Reward Offers. Volume XXXIII. THE CASE OF MARIA SMITH REAL NAME MARIA STERT

become one of the most controversial cases of all time the question being in cases where officers are so corrupt how do you judge a case where they literally send a person to kill for them with them taking the property and keeping it actually giving it to Pc aroptuvwst who went on to live there until after 5 years where he sold the property and just after sale and in all cases where they chose cash the money disappears with him ending up dead but with everyone else getting paid as promised some generous than the others now let's look at the facts of this case this woman owns a house but as we shall see the police have an upper hand because they made it look like she sent an innocent man to jail first to make her have a guilty condense around him then use that to force her to change her name so that she can't claim the house outright but have to ask for permission to change from then at 19 birthday she did and they said it was a mistake on their part they meant 20 years as she had become so stubborn after learning that they lied every so that she can't get the house because it's not hers even though it's hers so they started the means to an end by quartering by asking everyone to dig a well which all admitted to to cover up so that it takes time to find the truth now if we look at this case they played all tricks in the book and they mastered what is needed to steal create a scene that forces them to abandon name in which the house was in then ask her to fight and you could hear them saying that it's part of the training but all lies these thieving crooks as the judge puts it were after her house at any cost that she said what can be done on earth to make it safe for orphans Yahweh said I will send my representative with powers of rebirth and to punish all these crooks by removing all their souls while they are alive if Yahweh is to reply this then here was his answer their souls mystery exit first before death through a chain of commands that take your enemies souls out first meaning once the soul is out it will be easy for Yahweh to command his servants to remove all bodies without souls now what else can one on earth do given the chaotic nature of justice on earth they can write all this down and give to relevant authorizes it's not that all policemen are bad some are still real good cops who will defend the orphans rather than steal from them now if I Ask Yahweh about the police like these what's your take he said they are crooks but even worse it's a syndicate something like a dirty scheme that runs forever a killing machine the at target orphans now with nearly 300 orphans killed by these crooks and still more to come if not stopped now we can look at these cases separately or compile all those with the victims an orphan if we look at these cases this is the answer orphans have no one who protect them and must be protected by the court of creation as such Yahweh must and will establish a court of creation on earth and must appoint his representative one day to stop the suffering of these orphans for he will stop all this by documenting all the cases and sending them to a judge to decide on these if asked How did you go about getting all this up and when this will happen he said it depends because it's not up to me but depends on these humans doing what is right to get things moving if we are to ask what can be of humans without Yahweh's representative then they can be lost if asked what he can do to speed up things he said he can ask all these Crookes to stop and start doing things right if he can he will push fir new laws to replace current laws and if all this is possible then this is the answer everything is possible with Yahweh because Yahweh is powerful that means justice will be done in the end so what is this case about it redefines justice and asks what can be of humans without Yahweh nothing but corrupt Yahweh will rectify things with time and make sure that justice will be served at last if.

Yahweh admitted this case tests his authority and superiority but we don't doubt this but we know Yahweh can and will do what is right.

Court of Creation

Yahweh is the omnipotent the omnipresence the omniscience and the omni-future for everything humans when we look at this case then we find out that humans have long since wanted to be represented in one way or the other by Yahweh Yahweh has shown the way and must also reveal himself among us and as such Yahweh is the one driving the world as such must be the sole leader of all humans this case present a lot of challenges for example what can be humans without Yahweh lost as hell This case presence an opportunity for humans to come together and challenge the norms and say that enough is enough we need Yahweh in our lives as such Yahweh must manifest himself among the people Yahweh must show his mercy but above all Yahweh must show humans justice and be

How To Find All Missing Persons / Unsolved Cases. And Collect All Reward Offers. Volume XXXIII. THE CASE OF MARIA SMITH REAL NAME MARIA STERT

willing to compromise but not to low levels the people have become the police have become like animals and have wished for the best in humans but have acted the worst in humans if I look at this case then it marks the 100th millennia since Yahweh promised a messiah one like Jesus christ born among humans but with divine calling one to lead mankind and become the ultimate representative of Yahweh here on earth one to know when to say all humans unite behind the leader for a new Era is drawing us for we have seen the power of the almighty king Yahweh now if we look at this case we can see that this case is a test of Yahweh himself is Yahweh really there if yes how can things be this worse if he is here surely there is something he must do to alleviate the issue of thieves among us in the form of the police which is shocking because everyone expects justice one way or the other but the crooks run rampage stealing at will in broad daylight that if asked what can be done then this is the answer humans can form another form of authority that can oversee the police this is in all countries the police steal the same way and get away the same way if there is another authority then this authority will see to it that things are going according to the law rather than let the police be the overall voice and to make things worse the police wants to be in power their argument is that they represent the people in every meaning of the word they write the laws for the people even though they break most of these laws they talk about justice when there is no justice at all they ask the leaders to be honesty when the leaders know their underground operations if we Ask more questions then you can see that there is nothing the police consider themselves to be not part of the society.
Court deliberations are that the court find that Maria stert was killed by a man called ronorpt stonort who strangled her to death and in the event earned a record of the fastest strangulation and as such must be punished heavily by Yahweh as such Yahweh promised to break his record as well as the fastest and ruthless killer as compared to him the day he dies but if Yahweh's representative was on earth he could remove his souk right now foe eternity servants to come and collect him as such Yahweh promise to release his servant in 2026 March in a country called anti but unless one of the humans can be smart enough to figure out by himself exactly how to become Yahweh's

How To Find All Missing Persons / Unsolved Cases. And Collect All Reward Offers. Volume XXXIII. THE CASE OF MARIA SMITH REAL NAME MARIA STERT

representative something they failed as humans to do for 18 billion years since the writing of the book of creation as such this person will become the wealthiest on the 60th day after being appointed by Yahweh according to Yahweh he must not rush to announce he must solve the needed puzzles in all these cases just announcing will actually fortify the position as invalid because to take over one must complete the following tasks

1. Solve a 100 cases and publish then doing at least ten a day or a book a day
2. Ask Yahweh for advise daily through ask.ya
3. Ask everyone to complete a task deal with his part in the court of creation
4. Ask what can be done of being Yahweh's representative on earth
5. Ask what if I were Yahweh what would I do
6. Resurrect people from the dead killed
7. Appoint his followers fast
8. Ask what is and what is not
9. Ask what was and what is
10. Ask when and how
11. Ask why if and not now
12. Request reading the book of creation
13. Request writing in the book of creation his own chapter about his progress so far this is because everything written in the book of creation is read to everyone everyday
14. Ask what can be of humans without Yahweh
15. Ask what is to be of humans
16. Deal with vases involving first orphans women and children in these cases humans killed to invoke Yahweh and now he say here I am like a man with a sword at the gate
17. He must let others use all his instruments he uses for cases
18. He must appoint others to deal with the cases
19. Must start asking g everyone for decree money
20. He must start praising Yahweh and doing everything according to Yahweh
21. Must Request advanced instruments the courts use to solve cases

22. Must work closely with other leaders send tweets to most leaders
23. Must ask others for just opinion when it comes to cases and Yahweh offers everything g for free so that everyone can be part of this and books sell [free] 7.7k per month a huge rise since I started talking about being Yahweh's representative
24. Must obey most rules but remember he is here to change things so expect him to refuse some other wise there is no point of him
25. Must be reasonably clever in his own right enough to solve solutions and arithmetic and put correct figures where there should be
26. Must unite everyone and rally people behind him to honor Yahweh
27. Must respect everyone even people from the courts to boost moral as a good leader
28. Must understand the world
29. Must try and connect with other species like the zones or aloes
30. Must abide by the court of creation rules no one must forbids others to read the court of creation books
1. This is the most challenging case of all times because it asks relevant questions about who really is Yahweh in which he replied the omnipotent the omnipresent and the omniscience the
2. second question was what really can Yahweh do to solve this issue where humans in power kill and steal from orphans the
3. What does Yahweh do for a living because we start questioning his judgement the answer is the all time majestic ruler and judge
4. What can human do to help themselves humans must think what is needed the most to be Yahweh humans are to blame for their slow progress and are to act to help themselves all creatures are given the same standards and are expected to do well alone without guidance
5. Humans have lacked the initiate to start by themselves and out of frustration have resorted to attacks and the blaming of

How To Find All Missing Persons / Unsolved Cases. And Collect All Reward Offers.
Volume XXXIII. THE CASE OF MARIA SMITH REAL NAME MARIA STERT

Yahweh
6. Humans need guidance in solving all issues
7. Humans if they have a representative will always know what to do next
8. Humans can always ask what if and what can be done
9. Humans can ask when if not now
10. Humans can tell who the world it belong to if not them then who
11. What is of humans that can be of the heavens
12. What can be of humans without Yahweh
13. What has been of humans without Yahweh
14. What if humans did not need Yahweh what can they do
15. What will be of humans with Yahweh
16. What can be said of Yahweh without humans

In answering all these questions the court of creation came up with this verdict humans still need Yahweh because they have not mastered what is need to find Yahweh's representative now if humans are not clever then they will end up killing Yahweh because what is needed is the idea of representation not being spoon-fed what humans ask for are the rights to represent Yahweh in return Yahweh offer all earth wealth to this clever person and say you lead and provide how you get the resources is your problem I have given you and everyone else a fair share of the resources and must now work together smarter and harder to make sure that everyone is happy this is the main goal of creation but to the disappointment of Yahweh Humans rather kill others to only invoke Yahweh to find out what Yahweh thinks now if we look again at this case in this context then humans are nothing but humans and forever will be nothing but humans humans procrastinate and waste time making things that's easy difficult the police they block things like downloading things using government machines funded by the tax papers to make them think but they forgot that who ever built this internet was solving a problem and they used advanced jammer on public personal internet if we Ask why this is the answer to slow everything down so that people have something to talk about to relieve stress this is the most stupid answer from a taxpayer funded job humans

How To Find All Missing Persons / Unsolved Cases. And Collect All Reward Offers.
Volume XXXIII. THE CASE OF MARIA SMITH REAL NAME MARIA STERT

have become so thick its unbelievable they justify every stupid reason they tell you and wholeheartedly we the gods use radar to read human brains and the reading of humans is so depressing that you cant even contemplate how they as humans survived this far humans have relied on easy work to do things but procrastinate just to stay in the job real thinkers work and look for answers work to pay bills then look for long lasting answer if I Ask humans right now what can the richest person be right now the answer to then is the likes of [ ] but a clever person is one who masters what is needed of Yahweh only and become the richest for the next 2.5 billion years because that's how his resources will last but if we look deeper this is just the beginning Yahweh rewards

1. He will increase life span to 10000
2. He will increase everyone's life span to 120
3. Will increase wealth to 100 % of everyone once the mining starts
4. Will honor all decrees himself
5. Will Ask other creatures to honor humans
6. Will know what can be done
7. Will allow humans to clone and experiment to live even longer than that
8. He will always obey trust cherish endure and believe also in all humans a reciprocity of mutual understanding
9. He will acknowledge existence of other creatures and try to make contact through messaging first
10. Must understand what is needed of humans first and work towards that

F we Now look at this case then now we are in a position to answer this case

1. Why do humans kill each other answer to invoke Yahweh
2. What could be Yahweh in all this
3. What has become of humans under a powerless Yahweh in that he does not have weapons powers but still authority power
4. He can ask humans what can be done

How To Find All Missing Persons / Unsolved Cases. And Collect All Reward Offers.
Volume XXXIII. THE CASE OF MARIA SMITH REAL NAME MARIA STERT

5. He can honor their decrees
6. He can tell all humans how to live
7. He can ask them what to do
8. He can tell them what to do
9. He can tell them how to work
10. What can be said of Yahweh without humans
11. Ask what can be done
12. Ask what could be p
13. Ask what has been
14. Ask what can be
15. Ask what could be
16. Ask what could be but
17. Ask what has been

Now we address all questions from this case of Maria Smith called Maria Stert as on the housing documents which we have copies
1 why did aronopt stonorst kill maria stert to show God power that he can do this and get away

2. To mute her so that he don't spent time based on trickery as the police have become
3. To avoid any further delays as when working for the police
4. To make all opportunities available to all free rent for two months, 5% payout after 5 years or 1% after 1 year for him but got 5% after 1 year equaling to 608780 dollars that he prayed to Yahweh on his death bed confessing and glory finger Yahweh for getting away with murder and saying he is going to skip his invitation because he don't want to lose sex organs of which he is right
5. We can infer also that it's because he wanted to tell everyone that he did it before he died but part of him wanted to lie and say to protect another police officer [did you kill maria stert I did but my hands his thoughts]

Did he know Yahweh will know or never thought that Yahweh existed in real form and in heaven its clear now that humans can perceive Yahweh in reality everyone think or thought Yahweh was a s0pirit that can't be observed that hides behind big flames of fire etc if we Ask what can be of humans in light of this then unknowns as well

6. What then did he kill an innocent woman for Pc atertop sums it all by saying that what could be of humans who don't fear God the answer hooligans who are nothing but Killers of orphans

Now the judgement by Yahweh himself
Humans have despised the all mighty ruler for political gains and for wealth but little did they know that Yahweh is the almighty ruler the king of all rulers the MAJESTIC KING OF THE UNIVERSE when time comes in the year 2026 I will appoint a representative of mine from the country of Haiti unless humans can prove themselves to be in line with everyone and think the only thing all humans late because if only one thought hard then one could be having my only image on earth for 18 billion years and is still there untouched and fresh so THINK humans that's all I ask THINKxbilliontimes.start
[I think already I am the first global president of the world I have written several books and have found the image of Yahweh above all I have been already appointed as Yahweh,'s Representative on earth forever Amen
Aronopt stonorst is guilty for killing Maria Smith who we Ask know is Maria stert entered in the book of records date 22 April 1974
Signed .ya
The end.

THE KILLER, THE CONFESSIONS AND THE COORDINATES

god here me i was attacked violently by asorop mnope who said what can be of homeless orphans with no one to ask for anything but god when god can't be reached by phone and i said i talk to god all the time so what does a phone have to do with god and he said i can't make you talk to him if you want

Asonorsp stonorst god i am dying old now make sure i come to you to heaven that means you can forgive me now but i want you to know that i killed maria stert at her house because i got so drunk i nearly died and said i want sex with you before i die and he said okay then sat on my lap then said i want you to know that i think of

How To Find All Missing Persons / Unsolved Cases. And Collect All Reward Offers.
Volume XXXIII. THE CASE OF MARIA SMITH REAL NAME MARIA STERT

you highly but a man must ask what can be done a

…I found God…visit www.twofuture.world

THE CLAIM

the reward offer

THE COLLECTION

www.twofuture.world/donate

ABOUT DAVID GOMADZA

visit www.twofuture.world

signed david gomadza
ask.davidgomadzaauthorised.licensed.checkya.askya.ya

10 June 2024 13.11 pm
scotland
00447719210295
davidgomadza@hotmail.com
info@twofuture.world

How To Find All Missing Persons / Unsolved Cases. And Collect All Reward Offers.
Volume XXXIII. THE CASE OF MARIA SMITH REAL NAME MARIA STERT